MANDELA
Time To Be Free

Written by Sue Adler

Illustrated by Petra Röhr-Rouendaal

Edited by Bobby Joseph

Acknowledgements

My thanks to the many people who have helped and encouraged me with this book,
especially Babette Brown and Daniel Jones. Thanks also to the Open School, The History Archive,
SACHED, and The Workers' Library, all in Johannesburg. I am indebted to many books - and
would like to acknowledge the works of Fatima Meer, Mary Benson and of course
Nelson Mandela as major sources. S.A.

The Publishers would like to thank the following:
ANC, Anti-Apartheid Movement, Rashid Lombard, IDAF Photo Library,
Julie Frederikse, Hippograff Press, The Daily Rand, Shaun Harris and
Kano Mofokeng.

Every effort has been made to reach copyright holders.
The Publishers would be glad to hear from anyone whose rights they
have unknowing infringed.

Edited by Bobby Joseph
Design and layout by Jabu ka Mahlangu & Petra Rohr-Rouendaal

First published 1993 by Mantra Publishing Ltd
5, Alexandra Grove, London N12 8NU

This edition published 1997

Published by **Writers and Readers Publishing, Inc.**
P.O. Box 461, Village Station
New York, New York 10014

CONTENTS

This book is dedicated to the young people of South Africa who
are turning the pages of history even as you turn pages now *(B.J.)*
and to the memory of Ann Marie Davies *(S.A.)*
and to Helen and Theo Kotze who introduced me to the real
South Africa *(P.R-R.)*

Foreword

As a young person Nelson Mandela, like millions of others, was fired by a vision to create a world where all people could walk proud and free. Armed with the power of dreams, thousands of South Africans, many of them very young, worked to overthrow the oppressive system called apartheid. Many of these women, men and children paid the greatest sacrifice to make their dreams come true.

In April 1994 South Africans voted in the country's first non-racial and democratic elections. I myself, my friend and colleague Nelson Mandela and the majority of South Africans had our first experience of voting for the government of our country.

With the victory of the African National Congress and its president Nelson Mandela, the whole world saw a dream realised. In May 1994, Nelson Mandela became South Africa's State President in a new government of National Unity, and with great joy and celebration the dawn of a new South Africa was created.

The next stage in our fight for peace, justice and equality in South Africa has begun as, with President Mandela, we work to reconstruct and develop our beautiful country.

Walter M Sisulu
Deputy President, ANC

Let's start the story on Sunday 11th February 1990, when Nelson Mandela, the world's most respected and honoured political prisoner, was released after 27 years in prison.

On the wonderful day of his release, hundreds of thousands of people gathered to greet him in Cape Town, the city furthest south on the continent of Africa. A billion people all around the world watched on television. Not many people knew what he looked like; no one had seen a photo of him since he went to prison in 1964 as a tall, strong young man.

With his wife Winnie and his old friend Walter Sisulu, Mandela came to greet the huge crowd. He spoke to the people of South Africa and to the whole world, repeating words from his trial in 1964.

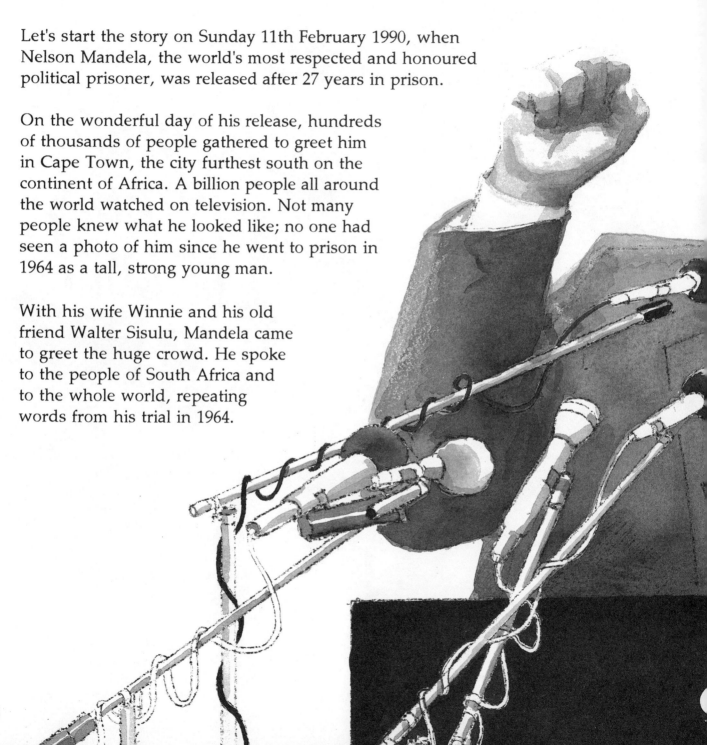

South Africa's all-white apartheid government thought Nelson Mandela was very dangerous. He was one of many people who fought against apartheid. Apartheid kept Black and white people apart in South Africa; it kept white people in power and Black people without rights and the vote.

The apartheid government stopped Mandela being seen and heard in his own country and throughout the world. Like hundreds of other men and women, he was banned, forbidden to go to meetings or even be with small groups of people. He was not allowed to write and speak about politics. He was imprisoned.

But in 1990, the actions of people in South Africa, young and old, helped by many outside, forced that same government to release Nelson Mandela. This was one part of the struggle against apartheid - a step towards freedom in South Africa. And in 1994 South Africans were free, at last, to vote. Most of them showed their support for Mr (soon to be President) Mandela.

What is apartheid?

This shows a school for Black children. This shows a school for white children - the apartheid government spent much more on every white child than on every African child.

That government spent more on health care for white children, too. Too many of our babies die from disease and malnutrition

But I thought apartheid was finished now.

Yes, it is. We have the vote and now all South Africans have a voice in their country. But the legacy of apartheid will be around for a long time.

It will take some time before the riches of this country are shared. It will be some time before my children have a good school to go to, good health care, a good house to live in with water and electricity - and before I have a good job.

13

The young Nelson Mandela

Nelson Rolihlahla Mandela was born near Umtata on 18th July 1918. His parents, Nonqaphi and Chief Henry Gadla Mandela, gave him both a Xhosa name and a heroic European name.

Nelson and his three sisters grew up in a small rural village in the Transkei. Then, the area was a 'reserve'. This means it was an area that the white government had set aside or reserved for Black people to live in.

The land, while beautiful, was not fertile. Many men had to leave to work in the cities and mines. Women and children and older men stayed on the land.

Although he was a member of the royal family of the Thembu people, Nelson, like most little boys in the African countryside, herded cattle and sheep and helped with the farming.

His father died when Nelson was just 12. Before his death, that wise man took his son to the Paramount Chief, saying, "This is my only son. I can say from the way he speaks to his sisters and friends that his inclination is to help the nation."

The Paramount Chief arranged and paid for Nelson to go to a mission school. It was difficult and expensive for Black South African children to study. Education was neither free nor compulsory for most South Africans.

At his new school, for the first time, Nelson came upon the ideas of white society. He was shocked to find that the books he was given to read told only of white heroes.

The stories he had heard at home about African heroes were not in any school books. Instead, these books described the African people as "savages" and "thieves".

Nelson did well at school, and went on to Fort Hare University. This university was one of the few places in South Africa for Black people to continue their studies. Here, Nelson met people who, like him, would one day be leaders of the people. One of these new friends was Oliver Tambo, later to become President of the African National Congress.

Nelson had to leave the University because he took part in a protest. He and many other students complained about their bad food, study and living conditions, and for this, they were punished.

He went back to the Transkei. The Chief was angry with him and ordered him to apologise to the University and return to his studies. He wanted Nelson to get married, with a plan that the young man would take over the chieftainship. But Nelson Mandela knew that this was not the life for him. He did not want to rule over an oppressed people. At the age of 22 he went off to the Transvaal, to the big city of Johannesburg.

Johannesburg, or Egoli - city of gold - was a new city. Just fifty years before Nelson went there, gold was discovered. Almost overnight, the city grew as the fortune-hunters rushed in. Gold was deep underground and Black miners were used by whites to get the treasure out of the earth. Black men came to work in the mines because the rural areas were very poor.

Soon the authorities made rules keeping Black families apart. The men worked in the new city; the women and children were not allowed to join them but had to stay in the country. They made rules to keep Black miners in unskilled and badly paid jobs. White people arriving from Europe to make their fortunes in South Africa had rights and privileges but Black South Africans had none.

The city Mandela saw was separated. People lived, travelled, played and worked apart. White and Black South Africans lived (and still live) in different parts of the city. Many white families have large and beautiful homes with gardens and swimming pools; Black people usually live in crowded conditions and poverty on the outskirts of the city in the townships.

A house in a white suburb.

Like all Black South Africans, Mandela needed a pass to work, to live in a township, and to travel. He also needed a job! Tall, strong and very fit, he was taken on to guard a hostel near a gold mine. Black men working on the mines had to stay in crowded hostels. Nelson worked the 'graveyard' shift, from ten at night to six in the morning.

He soon left his grim job and went to one of the parts of Johannesburg for Black South Africans – a township called Alexandra. There he met the man who would be his life-long friend, Walter Sisulu. Encouraged by him, Nelson returned to study law at the university in Johannesburg. And he met white and Indian people who opposed apartheid.

In 1944 Nelson married Walter's cousin, Evelyn Ntoko Mase. She was a nurse and her earnings helped to pay for Nelson's studies. The couple had three children, Thembelihle, Makaziwe and Makgatho. The family lived in a tiny house in Orlando, an area later named Soweto. But by 1953, Nelson had to pay a high price for his active life in politics. His marriage ended in divorce.

Housing in a township.

Mandela and the African National Congress

Walter Sisulu was a member of the African National Congress - the ANC - and soon Mandela joined too. These young men wanted to change the ANC, making it more in touch with the people. Nelson, Walter and their friends soon got support from many young women and men. Mandela was part of the Youth League, the group that made the ANC much more popular and lively. Leaders in the ANC, such as Govan Mbeki, recognised the values of the young men and shared their commitment. So, in 1949, the Youth League's programme of actions was supported by the ANC.

This was a time of change in South Africa. The all-white Nationalist Party government was one year old. It was determined to increase the separation of Black and white South Africans. It developed the system we call apartheid. The ANC Youth League organised a campaign of defiance, refusing to obey the government's many new laws which were designed to keep Black South Africans poor and without rights. Nelson was in charge of this campaign.

He was also elected Youth League President. In 1951 he was elected President of the ANC in the Transvaal, one of South Africa's four provinces. He was, as his father had said, a born leader. But, right away, the government banned him. Banning orders meant he was not allowed to attend meetings and was forbidden from leaving Johannesburg. Another ban forced him to resign from the ANC.

Like many others, Nelson Mandela defied his banning orders. He worked in a law office with Oliver Tambo in the city of Johannesburg, where they defended people in trouble. He spoke and worked in the townships. He wrote about the terrible laws that made life for Black South Africans so hard while most of white South Africans lived in the comfort and wealth apartheid gave them. Because he was banned all his actions were illegal.

Nelson Mandela was first imprisoned in 1952. This was because
he was at a meeting that went on past 11 o'clock at night. Black South
Africans needed a special pass, signed by a white person, to be
out late at night. Probably half of all Black South Africans have
been arrested for pass offences at some time in their lives.

Singing the ANC anthem, he and his comrades went off to jail - this time
for 15 days. As usual, the police were rough. One of the men arrested with
Mandela was pushed so hard by a white policeman that he fell and broke
his ankle.

Police brutality in South Africa.

South Africa: A history

Tell me a bit about South Africa's history— I think I need to know this to understand about apartheid and the struggle for freedom.

Many Black nations have lived in South Africa for centuries. Sotho and Xhosa people settled and lived in parts of what is now called South Africa from about 1000 AD. The Khoi-Khoi and San people lived in the southern part of South Africa - known to Europeans as the Cape of Good Hope. Their first contact with white people was in 1486, when Portuguese sailors landed in what we now call Cape Town.

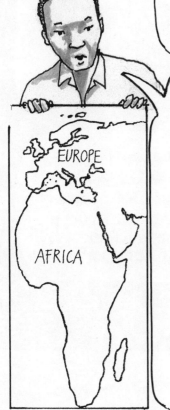

The first white settlement in South Africa began in 1652 when men from Holland arrived at the Cape. Within 20 years, these settlers were at war with the local inhabitants, the Khoi-Khoi.

About 150 years later, the British occupied the Cape of Good Hope. More than 10,000 Dutch people, known as Boers, left the Cape to avoid Britain's new anti-slavery laws and to keep their own way of life. They trekked north in search of land. They met and fought Nguni-speaking Africans. They settled in the Orange Free State and the Transvaal, provinces where, by the end of the 19th century, diamonds and gold were discovered.

Meanwhile, more British settlers came to live in South Africa. They brought labourers from India to work on sugar farms. Conflict between the two white groups - the Boers who spoke Afrikaans, and the English -- led to two wars. Eventually, the English won. In 1910 Britain allowed South Africa's four provinces to become a Union. African people had no political power, and no say in the way their own country was run.

African people organised together to fight racism and to fight for their place in the government of their country. This organisation, later called the ANC, protested at once to the British Government. They asked the British to take away the Land Act of 1913.

Whites claimed almost all the land for themselves with Acts of Parliament in 1913 and 1936. Black South Africans - most of the people - were allowed to buy or lease just 13% of the land. This land was 'reserved' for Black people.

This idea of reserving land gave Verwoerd, the prime minister of South Africa in the 1950s, his idea of Bantustans. These were areas, scattered around the country, that the government said were different countries. But Black South Africans and people outside South Africa did not accept this.

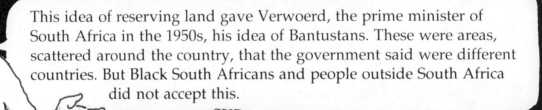

SOUTH AFRICA — THE BANTUSTANS

VENDA
LEBOWA
GAZANKULU
KA NGWANE
KWANDEBELT
BOPHUTHATSWANA
QWA-QWA
KWAZULU
TRANSKEI
CISKEI

Look at the map to see how little land we got; how it is dotted around the country in all the poorest parts. Can you see the Transkei, where Mandela was born?

Black leaders and workers organised peaceful protests and huge strikes – one example was a strike by African miners for better working conditions and pay. But protests and demonstrations could not stop apartheid developing.

In 1948 a new Afrikaans-speaking government was elected by the white people of South Africa. This all-white Nationalist government set out to make apartheid official policy and law. Everything - jobs, housing, schools, hospitals, buses, even park benches - were separate.

NIE-BLANKES

Non-whites

Europeans only

WHITES ONLY

Slegs vir Blankes

Non-whites only

BLANKES

Nelson Mandela and many others in the ANC, the Youth League, trade unions and other organisations protested and struggled against apartheid. Often, the government used violence to stop them. Moving people by force from their homes and killing peaceful demonstrators became part of the apartheid life. And African, Coloured and Indian South Africans were kept in low paid jobs, without the good schooling and health care that white South Africans enjoyed.

The all-white government decided for all the people - although it represented just a few of the people. The government did not want to know what most South Africans wanted. But outside the government people organised and opposed apartheid.
You will find out more about this on the next pages.

The Congress of the People

In 1954 a new organisation, The Congress Alliance, was formed from groups that opposed apartheid, including the ANC. The Alliance tried to find out what the people wanted for their future. Many were asked, "What kind of South Africa do you want to live in?"

Volunteers asked men in the mines, women who were domestic servants in white homes, women and men who worked in factories and on farms, children and their grandmothers living in the country. At a mass rally, the people's wishes were made into the Freedom Charter.

Mandela was still banned and could not speak at this enormous meeting. But he and Walter Sisulu were there in disguise.

Freedom Charter

We the People of South Africa, declare for all our country and the world to know that South Africa belongs to all who live in it, Black and white...

The people shall govern!
All national groups shall have equal rights!
The people shall share in the nation's wealth!
The land shall be shared among those who work it!
All shall be equal before the law!
All shall enjoy human rights!
There shall be work and security!
The doors of learning and of culture shall be opened!
There shall be houses, security and comfort!
There shall be peace and friendship!

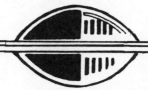

The Freedom Charter was a programme to guide South Africans to freedom. It showed a vision of a future, and better, South Africa.

Of course it frightened the apartheid government and made it angry. After collecting information and documents and planning for more than a year, the government hit back.

The Treason Trial and the 1950s

In the very early morning, before sunrise, police banged on the doors of more than a hundred people. They searched the houses, taking books and magazines - and in the end they arrested 156 people. Mandela was one of the people arrested and accused of high treason. These 156 people, Black, white and Indian South Africans, were accused of planning to overthrow the government, using violence.

The trial lasted for more than four years. Many of the leaders met each other for the first time and were able to get to know each other well.

In the end, everyone was found 'not guilty' and acquitted. There was no evidence that any of them had planned to use violence to end the apartheid regime.

Life went on while the trial was held. One day, Nelson was having a quick lunch in a cafe. Oliver Tambo and his fiance, Adelaide Tsukudo came in. "You must meet my friend Winnie," said Adelaide.

Winnie Nomzamo Madikizela was a social worker who stayed in the same hostel as Adelaide. Soon after meeting her, Nelson invited Winnie to lunch. "I was of course petrified - he was much older than me and he was a patron of my school of social work. So when I got this call, I couldn't work for the rest of the day," wrote Winnie in her book *Part of My Soul*.

The two went to an Indian restaurant. Winnie remembers the hot, hot curry - Nelson's favourite food - and the many people who came to speak with him during the meal. She saw that he really did belong to the people.

The next day, she saw Nelson again - this time while he was working out in a gym. She realised that he was so very busy that they would never have much time together alone. The trial, his work, meetings in the townships, all had to be fitted into the day. But one afternoon he said to her, "You know, there is a woman, a dressmaker, you must go and see her, she is going to make your wedding-dress. How many bridesmaids would you like to have?"

In June 1958 they were married in Pondoland, Winnie's home. Nelson had to get permission from the government to leave Johannesburg for four days. He was still on trial, and still banned. So they began their long marriage - 34 years as husband and wife, becoming parents of two daughters. But the family was rarely together. Apartheid and its laws forced Nelson and Winnie to live apart from 1960 to 1990.

Politics went on too. The ANC worked to make South Africa a democratic, multi-racial society. Some Black people disagreed and saw another way forward.

We shall think of co-operation with other races when we have come into our own.

They wanted 'Africa for Africans'. These people - called Africanists - did not agree with the Freedom Charter. At the Transvaal ANC Conference in 1958, the Africanists decided to split from the Congress. When Albert Luthuli, the President of the ANC, addressed the conference, he heard from an Africanist, "We want no co-operation with whites at this stage. We reject the Freedom Charter."

A group broke away from the ANC and formed a new organisation, the Pan-Africanist Congress (PAC). Robert Sobukwe, a university lecturer, was its President.

Turning Points

Sharpeville 21 March 1960

The PAC organised a demonstration, protesting against the pass laws. 20,000 people assembled in an empty field and burnt those hated pass books. As people sang, the police opened fire. They shot and killed 69 people, ten of them children. They injured more than 200. Many were shot in the back, as they turned and ran from the police.

This journalist wrote:

> One woman was hit about ten yards from our car. Her companion, a young man, went back when she fell. He thought she had stumbled. Then he turned her over and found her chest had been shot away. He looked at the blood on his hand and said, "My God, she's gone!" Hundreds of kids were running too. One little boy had an old blanket which he held up behind his head, thinking perhaps that it might save him from the bullets.

POLICE FIRE KILLS
69 AFRICANS

Rand
Daily Mail
Tuesday March, 22 1960

SHARPEVILLE
MASSACRE
69
KILLED

That same evening, police killed two people and injured 49 in Langa, a township near Cape Town.

The whole world was shocked by the violence of the police in South Africa.

Chief Luthuli, the ANC President, burned his own pass book in public a few days after these terrible massacres, and ordered a day of mourning. He was arrested and given a suspended sentence. In the next year,
this man was awarded the Nobel Peace Prize.
The world recognised him as a great man;
the government in his own country
called him a criminal.

The apartheid government tried to
stop all protest.

State of Emergency!
ANC and PAC
banned!

With this response, the government made legal peaceful protest illegal. For decades, Black South Africans had used non-violence to challenge the government's violent laws and actions. But with the Sharpeville and Langa massacres, the time of peaceful protest to apartheid was over.

A new organisation, Umkhonto we Sizwe (often called MK) or Spear of the Nation, was formed. It was the fighting arm of the people against the government and apartheid. MK attacked buildings not human beings.

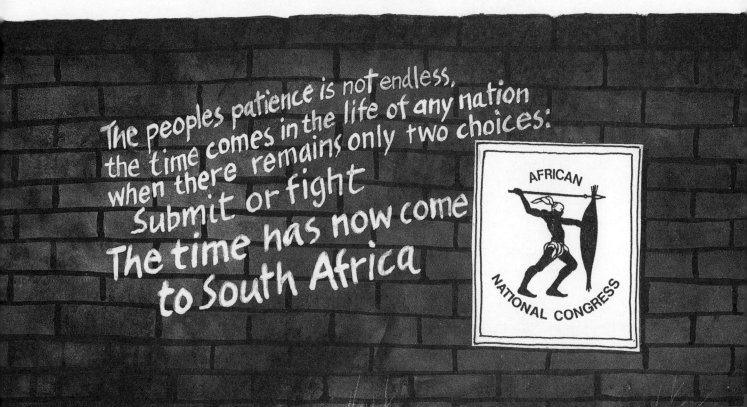

The peoples patience is not endless, the time comes in the life of any nation when there remains only two choices: Submit or fight The time has now come to South Africa

AFRICAN NATIONAL CONGRESS

On the run

As leader of MK and of the banned ANC, Mandela went underground. For a year and a half he lived 'on the run'. He could not stay at home with Winnie and their two small daughters. Sometimes, he was able to meet them in secretly at a friend's house in Rivonia, a white suburb in Johannesburg.

He had many disguises - a favourite was the hat and uniform of a chauffeur.

During this time, South Africa left the Commonwealth. It became a Republic. The government celebrated. Mandela protested. He helped organise a big, successful strike - a 'Stay at Home' as a protest against the apartheid state.

Nelson travelled outside South Africa. He met many leaders - Haile Selassie of Ethiopia, Julius Nyerere of Tanzania and Kenneth Kaunda of Zambia. He said, "For the first time in my life I was a free man."

On his return to South Africa, he broadcast on an underground station, Freedom Radio.

He went to a meeting in Durban, Natal. The police set up road blocks and caught Mandela, South Africa's Black Pimpernel.

Nelson Mandela was arrested. He managed to turn the case into a political trial. But the wonderful speeches he gave were not widely reported - the governments laws stopped his voice being heard; his words being read; his face being seen.

Nelson was sentenced to five years in prison, because he had encouraged people to strike, and because he had left the country without a passport. He was sent to Robben Island. Then, he was taken to Pretoria as one of the accused in the Rivonia Trial.

Rivonia Trial

Someone told the police that a big house in Rivonia, a quiet suburb of Johannesburg, was used by MK. Police raided the house, took thousands of documents and arrested Walter Sisulu and eleven other men. They transferred Mandela to Pretoria, to stand trial with his comrades. To start the defence, Mandela made a four hour speech. Calm and dignified, he spoke of the struggle for freedom. He explained the relationship between the ANC and MK and described the violence of the apartheid government. He spoke of the way white South Africans saw Black South Africans, and of his ideal for a free, democratic South Africa.

Whites tend to regard Africans as a separate breed. They do not look upon them as people with families of their own; they do not realise that they have emotions - that they fall in love like white people do; that they want to be with their wives and children like white people do; that they want to earn enough money to support their families properly, to feed and clothe them and send them to school.

The United Nations called for the release of the Rivonia trialists - men who fought for their country and took care that people were not killed or hurt in their actions against the government.

The eight men found guilty were sentenced to life imprisonment.
The Black men were sent to Robben Island; the white man was sent to Pretoria Jail.

Robben Island

This small rocky island is in the rough and shark-infested seas near Cape Town. It was used as a prison by the Dutch settler Jan Van Riebeeck in 1659. Here he imprisoned Autshumao, a Khoi-Khoi man, a fighter in the war between the Dutch and the Khoi-Khoi. Together with the San people, the Khoi-Khoi were the original inhabitants of the Cape and the first herders in Southern Africa. Autshumao, the first political prisoner of the island, was also the only one to have successfully escaped.

Robben Island, one of the most secure prisons in the world, was the home of hundreds of prisoners when Mandela and his comrades were sent there. The political prisoners had been teachers, doctors, factory and office workers, traders, lawyers and farm workers. Some were teenagers, others were men in their sixties. Some were ANC members. Some were PAC members. They all wanted to see real change in South Africa.

The Black men convicted at the Rivonia Trial were separated from the other prisoners. They were kept in an 'isolation block' with many tiny cells. Mandela's cell was about 4 square metres - a tiny space, especially for a big, tall man. There was a mat on the floor, and he had two blankets, and thin clothing - almost useless in the cold winter nights. He lived on the prison diet for all African prisoners - porridge, tasteless soup and black coffee.

Chained at the ankle and forced to stay silent, the prisoners dug, cut and carried stone. This was heavy, exhausting and useless work and Mandela soon protested to the wardens. Life and the fight for justice continued. Using hunger-strikes and making strong arguments to the wardens, the political prisoners gradually won the right to talk to each other, to get better food and clothing and to study.

Mandela gave so much help and encouragement to his fellow prisoners in their studies that Robben Island was jokingly called the Mandela University. But life on the island was tough. After a visit, Albertina Sisulu said to Winnie, "Oh, our men are shrinking here! But their spirit is strong."

Some stories from prison

Eddie Daniels, a member of the Liberal Party, tells this story. "Mandela taught me to survive. When I was ill, he could have asked anybody else to see me. He came to me personally. He even cleaned my toilet!"

Ahmed Kathrada, one of the Rivonia men, was with Nelson on Robben Island and, later, in Pollsmoor Prison in Cape Town. He wrote more than 8000 pages during his twenty-five years in prison telling of daily life. He tells this story about Mandela - the strong leader, and as we see, a kind, gentle man too. "There were these crickets making a terrible noise. We'd want to kill them. He'd go carefully and pick up a cricket. If the window was open he would let it out. But he would never kill, not even an ant, a cricket or a bee."

Indres Naidoo, an Indian comrade, wrote a book describing his ten years on Robben Island. He called it Island in Chains. He wrote this about Mandela: "Comrade Mandela - with him you had no choice, you had to respect him. There was something about his large, calm physical presence and assured thoughtful manner that carried people along; his manner of always approaching problems in a correct way and guiding us in solving our day-to-day difficulties."

Mandela and his family

Political prisoners, like Mandela, were allowed one short letter and one visit every six months. Because children over 2 and under 16 were not allowed to visit, he could not see his own children growing up. And since Winnie was imprisoned and put under house arrest, he did not even see her regularly. After five years in prison, he had just five visits, each lasting half an hour.

It was hard for the wives of the prisoners, too. There were times when Winnie and Albertina Sisulu were both banned because of their political actions. When they went to see their husbands, they were not allowed to travel together.

Nelson and Winnie's elder daughter Zeni married into the royal family of Swaziland. Because of this, she was allowed a 'contact visit' with her father. Until then, he had not been allowed to touch his visitors - his wife, his mother and his children. Zeni took her year old baby with her. Mandela was delighted to see and to be able to hold and cuddle his little grandchild.

Zeni and Zindzi Mandela,
growing up without their father

This poem by Nelson and Winnie's younger daughter Zindzi, was written when she was twelve years old. It describes the feelings of a child whose father is a political prisoner.

I stand by the gate
School's out
Smoke fills the location
Tears come to my eyes

I wipe them away
I walk into the kitchen
To see my mother's
Black hard-washing hands
A forceful smile from
A tired face

We sit and have supper
I pick up a picture of my father and look
My mother turns away
Tries to hide

My father held my mother
In his arms
He is roughly separated
From her

The van pulls away
Mother watches bravely enough
I as a child do
Not understand

My heart aches
How I long to see my father
At least to hold his hand
And comfort him
Or at least to tell him
He'll be back some day.

Nelson Mandela's mother died in 1968. She was a quiet woman who lived a humble life - yet her funeral was attended by thousands, and by hordes of police. Nelson had not seen her for years and was refused permission to go to her funeral. Three months after the funeral, Winnie was able to visit Nelson and tell him of his mother's illness and burial.

Nelson worried about the family he had to leave behind when he was sent to prison. When he was released, he said he was unhappy about leaving his family. Life was difficult for his wife and children.

While Nelson was in prison, Winnie Mandela, herself a political leader, was arrested, imprisoned and kept for a year and a half in solitary confinement. She was put under house arrest.

Banned by the government, she lost her job as a social worker and had to take low-paid work in shops and offices. When she did once manage to get a good job, she was quickly arrested again and put into prison.

In the 1960s and 1970s, Winnie had very little money for herself and the children. The government tortured and tormented her. They banished her to a small town in the Orange Free State, miles from family and friends, where she knew no-one. But they could not stop her fighting against apartheid.

Young people fighting for freedom

Afrikaans, the language of the ruling group of white South Africans, was made the language of teaching in Black secondary schools. Angry because they were forced to study in Afrikaans, children and their parents protested. Many pupils went on strike. In the township Soweto, 30,000 people gathered in a rally on 16th June 1976.

Children held banners saying: "If we must do Afrikaans, Vorster, the Prime Minister, must do Zulu."

Police fired on the children. Their first victim was 13 year old Hector Peterson. Police and the army, with their guns and weapons, went into townships all over South Africa.

In the terrible months following the murders at Soweto, more than 1,000 people, most of them young, were killed. What began as a children's demonstration became a national uprising. The people of South Africa went on strike, marched and rioted, showing their anger at the government.

Throughout the 1970s, the Black Consciousness Movement grew. Steve Biko, leader of South African Students Organisation, explained the need for Black people to join together and work as a group, getting rid of the chains that kept Blacks in the service of whites.

The apartheid government, just as it had jailed and banned the ANC and PAC leaders, jailed and banned Black Consciousness leaders. They arrested Steve Biko - and this strong young man died at the hands of the security forces when he was in prison.

Young leaders were killed; children who fought against apartheid were killed.

Steve Biko

A leaflet to parents read: "Be proud for giving birth to such heroic children. They have not died in vain and will continue the battle until victory is won.

Many young people left the country, to train and learn.

Still without rights

On Robben Island, prisoners were not allowed newspapers or radios. There was no television. But still, news of the world reached them.

Mandela heard of the Soweto uprising, and managed to smuggle a message out of his prison saying, "Unite! Mobilise! Fight On! We shall crush apartheid."

In l982, he and four other comrades from the Rivonia trial were moved from Robben Island to a prison in Cape Town called Pollsmoor. In this lonely little place they could not even see the countryside. They missed the other prisoners. But they were allowed some newspapers and could sometimes listen to the radio. Mandela knew that actions against apartheid grew in the 1980s.

He heard that people refused to pay rent when terrible increases occurred. He learnt that trade unions became bigger and stronger as more Black workers joined them.

He was also angry and distressed to learn about the increased powers given by the government to the police and the army. Huge numbers of people many of them young, were locked up in prison without trial.

Then in 1985, the State President P.W. Botha, offered to release Mandela - but only if he agreed to give up armed struggle.

Nelson Mandela refused to be released with those conditions. He made a statement, which his daughter Zindzi read. She mentioned Botha, and earlier Afrikaner government leaders.

My father says he is not a violent man. It was only when all other forms of resistance were no longer open to him that the MK turned to armed struggle... My father says Botha must show that he is different to Malan, Strijdom and Verwoerd. Let him renounce violence... Only free men can negotiate... My father cherishes his own freedom dearly but he cares even more for YOUR freedom. Too many have died since he went to prison... Your freedom and his cannot be separated. He will return!

Meanwhile, the ANC were still very busy. It had been banned since 1961, so it became an underground movement in South Africa. Outside the country it became an organisation - some say a government - in exile. Oliver Tambo was its President; and its headquarters were in Lusaka.

The ANC set up a school in Mazimbu, Tanzania.
It was called the Solomon Mahlangu College in honour
of a young MK fighter sentenced to death by the apartheid
government. Some of the children who had to leave their country
because of their (or their parents') actions against apartheid, went to
live and learn in Mazimbu.

Inside South Africa, violence continued
and many died. Often, their funerals
became the place for politics because the
State of Emergency of 1985 stopped meetings.
Funerals were one event where people could get
together; where they could discuss the government and
ways to struggle against the laws that kept them without
52 rights in their own country.

We are the Children of Africa

We are the children of Africa
And it's for freedom that we're fighting now.

A heavy load, a heavy load
And it will take some real strength.

Asikhathali noma si boshwa
Sizimisel' inkululeko.

Unzima lomthwalo
Ufuna madoda.

(Zulu language)

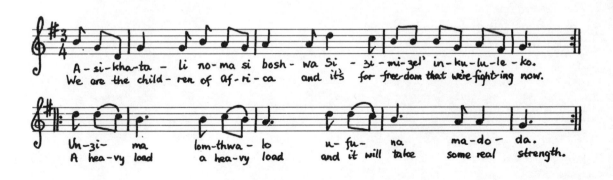

A-si-kha-ta - li no-ma si bosh - wa Si - zi-mi-zel' in-ku-lu-le - ko.
We are the child - ren of Af-ri-ca   and it's for free-dom that we're fight-ing now.

Un-zi- ma   lom-thwa - lo   u- fu- na   ma-do- da.
A hea-vy load   a hea-vy load   and it will take   some real   strength.

Free Nelson Mandela!

Meanwhile, the campaign to free Mandela went on around the world. Everywhere, except in South Africa, his name was heard in the streets. Songs were written about him, people wore badges and T-shirts saying: "Free Nelson Mandela".

Schools, roads, parks were named after Mandela. He became a legend in his own time; a hero to people fighting for freedom and a better, more equal, world.

Nelson Mandela's 70th birthday concert - Wembley June 1988

Back in South Africa, in 1989, a young man wrote, "I'm proud to be Black like Mandela" on his overalls. He was fired from his job, because Mandela was banned and could not be mentioned. Many others went to prison because they opposed the government. Many had the same ideas as Mandela and the ANC. They believed that South Africa should be a country where everyone had rights. They knew it was time to be free.

Then, in February 1990, the ANC, PAC, and other organisations were unbanned. Mandela and other political prisoners were released from jail. Mandela's release was watched all over the world. And all over the world, people were happy and excited as they saw that man step towards his own, and his country's, freedom.

Mandela was often on television. For the first time in years, you could say his name, listen to and read his words, discuss his ideas without losing your job or going to prison.

President Mandela

At the first ANC conference inside South Africa for 30 years, people met to discuss plans for the future South Africa and to vote for their leaders. Nelson Mandela was elected President of the ANC; Walter Sisulu was elected Deputy President. The ANC looked forward to governing South Africa soon.

There was much to be done before "one person, one vote" elections could take place. Mandela had the key role in talking with the Nationalist Government's President, F W de Klerk. The two men were awarded the Nobel Peace Prize in honour of their work towards creating a new South Africa.

But violence continued in the early 1990s. Many, many people were killed before they could see peace in their land. The apartheid government's support of Zulu leader Buthelezi and his Inkatha Freedom Party was one source of the terror; police action another. Apartheid, based on inequality and the division of people, encouraged anger, hatred, and terror. There was fierce fighting in parts of South Africa and people feared there would be civil war throughout the land.

For nine months in 1992, the ANC stopped its talks with President de Klerk and the Nationalist Government. People demonstrated to show they wanted peace, the vote and freedom.

Despite the fighting, fear and actions of those who did not want a democratic South Africa, the event that many had dreamed of, and many had died for, finally happened.

In April 1994, all adult South Africans, Black and white, went to vote in their country's first-ever democratic elections.

59

What happened then?

It took a while to count all the votes but then we sang and danced because of the ANC victory; because of the end of the white power.

Suddenly all South Africans were happy. The election went peacefully.

We got a new government of National Unity...

ANC 62.7%
Nationalist Party 20.4%
Inkatha Freedom Party 10.5%

PAC 1.2%

Other Parties 5.2%

President de Klerk made a fine speech when he knew his party had lost. He congratulated Nelson Mandela.

He said: "Mr Mandela has walked a long road and now stands at the top of a hill. A traveller would sit down and admire the view. But a man of destiny knows that beyond this hill lies another and another. The journey is never complete. As he contemplates the next hill, I hold out my hand to Mr Mandela in friendship!"

On 10th May 1994 Nelson Mandela became South Africa's first Black president. Thabo Mbeki was sworn in as Deputy President and F W de Klerk as Second Deputy.

I stand before you filled with deep pride and joy - pride in the ordinary people of this country...You can loudly proclaim from the rooftops - **FREE AT LAST** !

Mandela spoke solemnly to the crowd and the world's television cameras at his formal ceremony in the gardens of Pretoria's government buildings He said, "Never again and never again shall it be that this beautiful land will again experience the oppression of one by another and suffer the indignity of being the skunk of the world."

There as a jazz band played, Nelson Mandela moved towards the people, smiling and dancing a little, enjoying his great moment.

My Hero Mandela

My hero stands over the valley of his people

fighting for them with no spear, no gun, no knife

only the weapon of mouth and knowledge,

his head held high. The grey haired man walking out

of prison not sad, not full of hatred and revenge

but smiling, laughing, laughing

the laughter of his people.

There he is, the man who

was imprisoned but smiling

and forgiving. There is my

one and only Mandela.

My hero, Mandela!

by Kano Mofokeng
(10 year old South African schoolboy)

Now in the eighth decade of his life and separated from Winnie, President Mandela, hero to many in the world, works as hard as ever. His autobiography tells of the "Long walk to freedom". Responsibilites come with freedom, and, he writes, "my own long walk is not yet ended." 1994 welcomed a new government, a new president, a new flag and a new national anthem in South Africa - but old problems remain.

There is still terrible poverty in this rich land. Millions of South Africans still have no jobs. There is a lot of crime. Many houses are without water and electricity. More than half of South Africa's adults have not had the chance to learn to read and write. South African children - like you - need good education and real opportunities to make their futures secure and happy.

One of the first actions taken by the new Government of National Unity was to set out a programme to change, develop and unite South Africa and sort out the mess left by apartheid.

Before the historic election, Mandela said, "I wish all South Africans not simply the hope of peace and goodwill but a new era in which these ideals will be a lasting reality." When millions of people in South Africa voted for Nelson Mandela, the new era began.

NKOSI SIKELEL'I-AFRIKA

Glossary

Amandla - "power" in Xhosa and Zulu. It is used to say: "Power to the People"

Ban - to stop a person or an organisation from taking action

Cape Town - South African city

Comrades - people who work together in the struggle for freedom

Democracy - political system where everyone has the right to vote for a government

Exile - forced to live outside your country

House arrest - a form of imprisonment. People in South Africa under house arrest could not leave their homes at night. They could not have more than one visitor at a time

Johannesburg - South African city

Location - another word for "township"

Nationalist Government - the all-white government in power from 1948 - 1994

Nguni - language grouping which includes Xhosa, Zulu and Ndebele languages

Nkosi Sikelel l'Afrika - *God Bless Africa* - first words of the ANC anthem and now one of the South African national anthems

Paramount Chief - the highest chief

Pass, Passbook - document which all Africans over 16 in South Africa had to carry (until 1986)

Pretoria - South African city

Solitary confinement - to be kept in a prison cell all alone

Soweto - township outside Johannesburg

Township - area on the outskirts of a city or town where many urban Black South Africans live

Treason - betrayal of the government/state

Xhosa - one of the nations of African people in South Africa. Mandela is a Xhosa - and the first language he spoke is Xhosa too

Zulu - one of the nations - and languages - of African people in South Africa

Index